"I'll do it!"

TAKING RESPONSIBILITY

Brian Moses and Mike Gordon

HODDER
Wayland

an imprint of Hodder Children's Books

The VALUES series:

"EXCUSE ME" LEARNING ABOUT **POLITENESS**
"I DON'T CARE!" LEARNING ABOUT **RESPECT**
"I'LL DO IT!" TAKING **RESPONSIBILITY**
"IT WASN'T ME!" LEARNING ABOUT **HONESTY**

Editor: Sarah Doughty
Designer: Malcolm Walker

First published in Great Britain in 1997 by
Wayland (Publishers) Ltd
Reprinted in 2001, 2002 and 2003 by Hodder Wayland,
an imprint of Hodder Children's books
© Hodder Wayland 1997

Hodder Children's Books, a division of Hodder Headline Ltd
338 Euston Road, London NW1 3BH

British Library Cataloguing in Publication Data
Moses, Brian, 1950 –
"I'll do it!": learning about responsibility. – (Values)
1. Responsibility – Juvenile literature
I. Title II. Gordon, Mike, 1948 –
170

ISBN 0 7502 2137 2

Printed and bound by G. Canale & C. S.p.A., Turin

CONTENTS

Are you a responsible person?

Can you be trusted to do things
on your own?

Do you:

clean your room ...

pick up your toys ...

Or do you say that you will
do these things, do them
badly or not do them
at all?

Learning to be responsible begins with being responsible for yourself, what you do and how well you do it.

Do you have to be reminded to:

comb your hair ...

and clean your teeth?

Do you wait until your mum
turns red in the face and
SHOUTS out loud?

Or do you think
about these things
yourself and
make sure
they get
done?

If you take responsibility for a few small jobs around the house, this can be very helpful.

From today onwards:

... you could make your bed

... you could water the plants

... and you could keep
your room tidy!

Sometimes you might be asked to be responsible for someone else ...

Quick, grab your brother and look after him while I talk on the phone, please.

When someone isn't feeling very well or has had an accident, they'll be glad to know that you will help.

Taking responsibility for your pets is a sign that you are really becoming a responsible person.

Make sure that you remember to feed them each day.

Clean them out yourself, but make sure you don't lose them around the house.

How well you take care of things is also a sign of how responsible you are.

Anything left lying around can easily get damaged, so remember to put books back on the shelves.

Put your cassette tapes away in their boxes.
If you don't, they can easily be unwound ...

You also have a responsibility to treat expensive equipment with great care.

Remember to wipe your hands clean before you start using the computer.

And don't put drinks anywhere
near the keyboard.

Being sensible in shops or in the street is another sign that you are becoming a responsible person.

When they see that you are really behaving responsibly, your parents may ask you to run errands for them ...

I don't want to drag these heavy bags into that shop. Can you nip in and get a paper, please. I'll watch you from here.

You will also need to learn to take responsibility for your possessions.

If you take your favourite toy with you to the café then you must remember to bring it home again.

Make sure you remember your ballet shoes, or your football kit, or your karate outfit after you've had a lesson.

Don't leave them sitting around in the cloakroom. They can easily get lost.

When you are at school, your teachers will notice if you can behave sensibly and they will give you important jobs to do:

... taking the register to the school office

... keeping the library books tidy

... making sure the
pencils are sharpened

... taking care of the goldfish.

Once you know that you can be responsible for yourself and your actions, then everyone will trust you with important jobs to do.

They will see that you are growing up and becoming a responsible person.

So how are you doing so far?

How high would you score on the RESPONSIBILITYOMETER?

A REALLY RESPONSIBLE PERSON

You've ALMOST MADE IT

QUITE RESPONSIBLE

TRYING HARDER

NOT VERY RESPONSIBLE

NOTES FOR PARENTS AND TEACHERS

Read the book with children either individually or in groups and then ask them the questions on pages 4/5. Talk about the answers they give you about being responsible for yourself. Can children honestly say that they clean teeth or have a wash without being asked to do so?

Ask children to list any jobs in the home for which they take responsibility. What happens if they forget to do the job? Some children might like to write a story about something that happens when they forget their responsibilities. Perhaps little brother wanders off and gets lost or maybe the rabbit escapes because the hutch is left unlocked.

Children can be asked to work out the differences between responsible and irresponsible behaviour with regard to a number of situations; e.g. you are staying the night with grandma but she falls down and can't reach the phone. What do you do? A dog starts running around the school playground, jumping up and barking at children.What would you do? You have wandered off in the supermarket and now you can't find your mother. What should you do? Various other situations can be devised, discussed and where appropriate, acted out, so that children can begin to consider responsible behaviour.

Talk about responsibility towards pets. Can children draw up a list of rules for looking after animals? What happens if the rules are broken?

Can children remember occasions when they have mislaid treasured possessions? Where were they lost? Were they found again? Tell the story of a lost toy abandoned in a café or left on a bus. What sort of adventures does the toy have and is it ever reunited with its owner? Read 'Dogger' by Shirley Hughes (see book list).

Explore the notion of responsibility further through the sharing of picture books mentioned in the book list.

The above ideas will help to satisfy a number of attainment targets in the National Curriculum Guidelines for English at Key Stage 1.

BOOKS TO READ

Monster and Frog Mind the Baby' by Rose Impey (Collins Picture Lions,1994)
Monster's sister goes out and leaves Monster in charge of her baby. This is quite a responsibility for Monster. The baby starts to cry but Monster's friend Frog calls round and has lots of ideas for calming her.

'After the Storm' by Nick Butterworth (Collins Picture Lions, 1992)
Percy the Park Keeper's animal friends all lose their homes in the Great Storm, and Percy, in his role as guardian of the park and its residents, sets out to help them create new habitats.

'Dilly and the Pirates' by Tony Bradman (Mammoth)
This contains the story 'Dilly and the Surprise Party' where Dilly the Dinosaur is given the responsibility of taking care of his little cousin in the hope that this will stop him behaving badly.

'Dogger' by Shirley Hughes (Red Fox)
The story of Dave and his special toy Dogger which is lost and then found again.

'An Evening at Alfie's' by Shirley Hughes (Collins Picture Lions, 1984)
Alfie and his babysitter, Maureen discover a leaking pipe and Alfie shows just how responsible he can be in a difficult situation.

INDEX